THE NORTHERN HOME FRONT
OF THE CIVIL WAR

ROBERTA BAXTER

Heinemann Library
Chicago, Illinois

www.heinemannraintree.com
Visit our website to find out more information about Heinemann-Raintree books.

To order:

☎ Phone 888-454-2279

💻 Visit www.heinemannraintree.com to browse our catalog and order online.

©2011 Heinemann Library
an imprint of Capstone Global Library, LLC
Chicago, Illinois

Edited by Megan Cotugno
Designed by Ryan Frieson
Illustrated by Mapping Specialists, Ltd.
Picture research by Tracy Cummins
Originated by [select]
Printed in [select]

14 13 12 11 10
10 9 8 7 6 5 4 3 2 1

6299

Library of Congress Cataloging-in-Publication Data

Baxter, Roberta, 1952-
  The northern home front of the Civil War / Roberta Baxter. — 1st ed.
      p. cm. — (Why we fought, the Civil War)
  Includes bibliographical references and index.
  ISBN 978-1-4329-3911-3 (hc)
  1. United States—History—Civil War, 1861-1865—Social aspects—Juvenile literature. 2. Northeastern States—Social conditions—19th century—Juvenile literature. 3. United States—Social conditions—To 1865—Juvenile literature. 4. United States—History—Civil War, 1861-1865—Juvenile literature. I. Title.
  E468.9.B29 2011
  973.7'1—dc22
                        2009050015

Acknowledgments

The author and publishers are grateful to the following for permission to reproduce copyright material:

Corbis pp. 4, 31, 43 (© Bettmann), 15 (© Hulton-Deutsch Collection), 41 (© Corbis); Library of Congress Prints and Photographs Division pp. 7, 8, 9, 11, 25, 30, 34, 35, 36, 37, 39, 40; National Archive pp. 20, 21, 24 top, 24 bottom (War & Conflict CD), 23 (Charters of Freedom); The Art Archive pp. 14 (Gift of Hon Irwin Untermeyer / Museum of the City of New York), 22, 42, (Culver Pictures); The Granger Collection, New York pp. 13, 17, 18, 19, 27, 28, 29, 33.

Cover of New York City during the Civil War reproduced with permission from Corbis (© Corbis).

We would like to thank Dr. James I. Robertson, Jr. for his invaluable help in the preparation of this book.

Every effort has been made to contact copyright holders of any material reproduced in this book. Any omissions will be rectified in subsequent printings if notice is given to the publisher.

All the Internet addresses (URLs) given in this book were valid at the time of going to press. However, due to the dynamic nature of the Internet, some addresses may have changed, or sites may have changed or ceased to exist since publication. While the author and Publishers regret any inconvenience this may cause readers, no responsibility for any such changes can be accepted by either the author or the Publishers.

Contents

Why Did We Fight the Civil War? 4

Why Did the South Secede? 6

Who Led the North? 8

What Was It Like to Live on a Northern Farm? 12

What Was Life Like in a Northern City? 14

What Was Life Like on the Frontier? 18

Who Protested Slavery in the North? 20

Will These Inventions Work? 24

What Were the Words and Music of the Home Front? 26

What Other Effects Did War Have on the Home Front? 28

How Did the Civil War End? 36

Can the Country Be Reunited? 40

Timeline 44

Glossary 46

Find Out More 47

Index 48

Throughout this book, you will find green text boxes that contain facts and questions to help you interact with a primary source. Use these questions as a way to think more about where our historical information comes from.

Some words are shown in bold, **like this**. You can find out what they mean by looking in the glossary, on page 46.

Why Did We Fight the Civil War?

When we think of the Civil War, we think of soldiers fighting in battles. But the war also changed the lives of the people back home. People of the North faced **economic** difficulties, struggled to manage farms without the men, and saw their homes and farms damaged by passing armies. Rising prices affected everyone, but especially **immigrants**, who usually had the lowest-paying jobs. Some Northerners profited from the war because of the need for crops and other wartime supplies for the **Union** army.

Slavery and States' Rights

Maintaining slavery and **states' rights** were the two biggest issues used in the South when arguing to **secede** from the Union. People and politicians had disagreed about slavery for years. There were slaves even in the North, and had been since before the **Revolutionary War**. Southern leaders wanted to be able to expand slavery into the new states that were forming from western territories. Northern leaders wanted to stop the expansion. Some people of the North wanted to get rid of slavery everywhere.

Southern plantations had large workforces of slave labor, unlike the small family farms of the North.

The two parts of the country also disagreed on states' rights. Leaders of the South believed that since the states had formed the Union, it was also their right to decide to leave the Union. Leaders of the North wanted to keep the Union intact, with all of the states included.

Greater Population

The white North had four times the population of the white South. The North also had seven times as many industrial firms. Massachusetts alone produced more factory goods than the entire South. As the war continued, people moved west to homestead on new farms and work in gold and silver mines. Immigrants continued to move to cities in the North and to farms across the country. The difference in population and production between North and South had a huge impact over the course of the war.

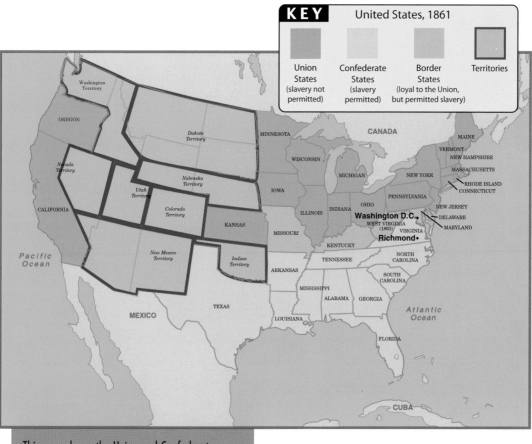

This map shows the Union and Confederate States during the Civil War.

Why Did the South Secede?

Over 40 years, several **compromises** were made in Congress to keep the **Union** together. These compromises did not entirely please the North or the South, and eventually no more compromises could be passed. The people of the South felt that the North intended to strangle their **economy** by passing laws against slavery.

A trio of senators, two from the South and one from the North, became famous for their attempts to save the Union. Henry Clay of Kentucky, John C. Calhoun of South Carolina, and Daniel Webster of Massachusetts worked out the deals for the compromises of 1820 and 1850.

Presidential Election

When the 1860 election for president came, the Democratic Party was split between candidates. Each candidate got votes, but not as many as the candidate of the opposing party. That party was a new party, the Republicans, who nominated Abraham Lincoln as their only candidate. Lincoln was elected, and the South felt he would vigorously push to free slaves and further destroy their way of life. The South was now determined to secede and form its own country.

On December 20, 1860, South Carolina seceded. By May 1861, eleven Southern states had seceded from the Union. These states formed the **Confederate States of America**.

COMPROMISES BEFORE THE CIVIL WAR

- Missouri Compromise of 1820: Missouri was admitted to the Union as a slave state, but a line was drawn so that slavery would not be permitted in any new states formed from land north of Missouri's southern border.

- Compromise of 1850: California was admitted as a free state; the territories of New Mexico and Utah could make their own decision about slavery; and a new **fugitive** slave law strengthened the search for runaway slaves.

- Kansas-Nebraska Act: Kansas and Nebraska were to decide for themselves whether or not to allow slavery.

Henry Clay was one of three key senators responsible for the compromises of 1820 and 1850, which kept the Union together a bit longer.

Who Led the North?

Abraham Lincoln was president of the United States during the Civil War. In speeches before the election in 1860, Lincoln said that the **Constitution** could not stop slavery where it already existed, but he pledged to keep it from spreading. "On that point," Lincoln said, "hold firm, as with a chain of steel."

Lincoln took office on March 4, 1861. Southern states had already **seceded** from the Union, and a month later, the Civil War began.

Early Life

Lincoln was born on February 12, 1809, on a farm in Kentucky. His family later lived in frontier Indiana and Illinois.

Lincoln's mother died and his father remarried. They lived in a one-room log cabin. Lincoln borrowed books from anyone who had some and spent his evenings reading by firelight. He attended school when he could. His father was a great storyteller, and Lincoln learned this talent.

**Primary Source:
Portrait of Abraham Lincoln**

Lincoln faced a divided nation in crisis when he took office in March 1861.

Thinking About the Source:

What do you notice first about this portrait of Lincoln?

This portrait of Lincoln was actually taken in 1865, ten weeks before his assassination.

Knowing this, do you view the portrait differently? Why?

Lincoln grew up in a one-room cabin, reading what he could find in his spare time.

Politics

Lincoln enlisted in his state **militia** during the **Black Hawk War**, but he never fought in a battle. He was elected to the Illinois **General Assembly** in 1834 and served for eight years. He studied law and earned his lawyer's license in 1836. Still intrigued by politics, Lincoln ran for the **U.S. House of Representatives** two times, but was defeated. Then in 1847, he was elected as a representative and served two years.

When Lincoln decided to run for the **U.S. Senate**, his opponent was Stephen Douglas. During the campaign, Lincoln spoke eloquently during debates with Douglas. In his acceptance speech as a candidate for senator on June 16, 1858, Lincoln said, "I believe this government cannot endure permanently half slave and half free. I do not expect the Union to be dissolved—I do not expect the house to fall—but I do expect it will cease to be divided. It will become all one thing, or all the other."

President in a Difficult Time

On November 6, 1860, Lincoln was elected president of the United States. In his first **inaugural speech**, Lincoln said that he believed the country should stay united. But his wish was not to happen. Soon after, four more states **seceded**.

During the Civil War, Lincoln was criticized for using the powers of the presidency without always consulting Congress. He chose the generals to lead the armies, read their reports, and visited them in the field. Sometimes the generals he picked were not the ones that Congress would have chosen.

In July 1863, Lincoln faced a threat to the country and his presidency. Men drafted to serve in the army rioted in New York. Most of the rioters were poor men who believed the **draft** hit them harder than those who could pay to get out of it. Protest marches were held but turned ugly. Blacks became the target of the mob's rage, and many were attacked on the streets. Lincoln sent units from Grant's army to stop the disorder.

In 1864, Lincoln was elected to a second term in office. His new vice president was Andrew Johnson.

TIMELINE OF ABRAHAM LINCOLN'S LIFE

February 12, 1809	Born in Kentucky
1832	Enlisted in state **militia**, never fought a battle
1836–1842	Served as Illinois legislator
1836	Passed bar exam to be a lawyer
1847–1849	Served in **U.S. House of Representatives**
1858	Debated Stephen Douglas during race for **U.S. Senate**
1860	Elected president of the United States
January 1, 1863	Issued **Emancipation Proclamation**
November 19, 1863	Gave Gettysburg Address
April 14, 1865	Shot by John Wilkes Booth, died the next day

First Lady Mary Todd Lincoln suffered the loss of her son Willie during the Civil War.

MARY TODD LINCOLN

In 1842, Lincoln married Mary Todd, the daughter of a **plantation** owner in Kentucky. Because her family owned slaves, some suspected Mary of having Confederate loyalties during the war. The couple had four sons, but only one lived to adulthood. One, Willie, died while his father was president. He probably had typhoid fever. His parents mourned for him, but Lincoln had to continue to lead the country.

What Was It Like to Live on a Northern Farm?

Even though the North had large cities, more than half of the people lived on small farms. Men worked in the fields and cared for animals. Most farmers raised grains such as wheat, corn, oats, and barley as their **cash crops**. They also grew potatoes, apples, and hay for animal feed, and raised cattle, pigs, and cows for meat and milk. Farms were about 60 to 100 acres. Farmers worked 12 to 15 hours a day during the spring and summer. At harvest time, they helped their neighbors with harvest in exchange for assistance with their own crops.

Women and Children

Women cleaned the house, cared for the children, sewed and mended clothes, and tended the garden and chickens. Much of the food eaten was preserved from the garden and orchard. Bread and butter were made at home, as were clothes for the family.

Children also had daily chores, including gathering eggs, helping care for younger children, feeding animals, and pulling weeds out of the garden.

Mechanical Helpers

Farmers began to use machinery in the North before the Civil War. In 1830, Cyrus McCormick developed a mechanical reaper that was used to cut and harvest grain. Other machines included planters and mowing machines.

With western farms included, the Union grew more wheat in 1862 than the whole country had produced in 1859. The farms managed to feed the people and soldiers of the North and export grain to Europe.

Items from the South, such as tobacco, cotton, and sugar, became expensive in the North during the war. Many people just stopped using tobacco or sugar. To make up for the loss of cotton, farmers raised sheep for their wool.

A typical Northern family farm is pictured here.

What Was Life Like in a Northern City?

The cities of the North were large. Men in cities worked as lawyers, doctors, and merchants. Bankers carried out business daily on Wall Street in New York City.

The North had hundreds more factories than the South. These factories made everything from rifles and cartridges to shoes and uniforms for the troops. Some people became wealthy from war profits and built large homes. They had all the newest conveniences, including gas lighting and steam heat.

Industry

In cotton mills, female employees worked hours at mechanical looms, making cloth. As the war continued, many mills began processing wool because cotton was scarce. Women earned less than men, so their work was more profitable for the mill owners. They worked extremely long hours. Children also worked in the Northern factories, which Southerners liked to point out when defending slavery.

Businessmen and bankers gathered each weekday on Wall Street in New York City.

Another thriving industry in the North was shipping. Ships left the harbors of New York City and Boston, Massachusetts, daily on voyages that often lasted years. Ships also docked daily, bringing items from around the world. During the war, grain shipments to Europe increased, and owners of ships earned good profits.

By the 1860 **census**, nine of the ten largest cities in the country were in the North. New Orleans, Louisiana, was the only Southern city in the top ten.

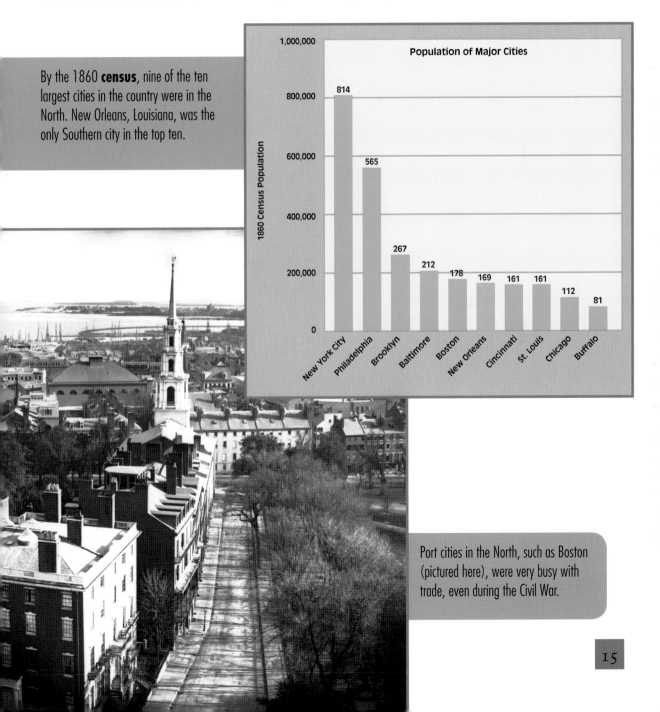

Population of Major Cities

1860 Census Population

City	Population
New York City	814
Philadelphia	565
Brooklyn	267
Baltimore	212
Boston	178
New Orleans	169
Cincinnati	161
St. Louis	161
Chicago	112
Buffalo	81

Port cities in the North, such as Boston (pictured here), were very busy with trade, even during the Civil War.

Immigrant Life

Immigrants still came to the U.S. during the Civil War. They often lived in **tenements** in the cities and barely managed to survive with the jobs they could find. In 1863, one count showed that half of New York City's population lived in tenements. Many families lived with 8–10 people crowded into one room, with no bathroom facilities other than a trench outside the door.

The crowded conditions allowed disease to spread rapidly. Typhoid, smallpox, measles, diphtheria, and scarlet fever killed many children.

Crime and Violence

Another consequence of the crowding was crime and violence. Sometimes the violence was directed at certain ethnic groups. The Irish had immigrated to New York in great numbers, and they were often accused of violence that they had not done. Sometimes fights would break out between ethnic groups. Often the immigrants were denied jobs based on their background. The ones that found jobs were often the lowest-paid employees.

Immigrants often lived close together in a section of town. Cincinnati, Ohio, had its German area, marked by German restaurants and signs in German.

Jobs for Immigrants

Some immigrants left the cities to try their luck in the Midwest. They worked on farms and in small towns and often became leading citizens. Many immigrants joined the Union army, where they would be paid $13 a month.

There was a fear among immigrants that freed blacks would compete with them for jobs. At the time of the Civil War, only about one percent of the population of the North was black. Most of these free blacks lived in tenements in the large cities.

Primary Source:
New York Tenements

Tenement homes were poor and very crowded. Pictured above is a wood engraving of a funeral on Baxter Street in Five Points, New York City.

The engraving was printed in a German-language American newspaper in 1860.

Thinking About the Source:

Describe everything that you see in this image.

What types of details do you notice in particular?

If this image were created today, what would be different?

What Was Life Like on the Frontier?

The frontier of a country is an area that has not been settled. It is a section with few people and towns. In 1862, Congress passed the Homestead Act, aimed at helping families settle the western frontier. The act said that a farmer could own 160 acres of government land if he made improvements, such as building a house and barn, and worked the land for five years. The only cost was a fee of $18. This was just the chance that many families wished for.

Sod houses were common on the western frontier.

Wagon Train West

Families began trekking west in wagon trains. The trip was over 800 kilometers (500 miles) and usually took two months.

When they found a suitable plot, they would file a claim. Then they built a house and barns. In the plains, trees were scarce, so houses were often made out of **sod**. Fields were plowed and planted. Settlers burned buffalo chips—dried poop—as fuel because of the lack of wood.

During the war, more than 2.5 million acres of land was homesteaded, adding nearly 15,000 new farms. Those farms produced grain, which was used to feed the Union armies and the people of the North. The excess was shipped to Europe.

Dreams of Gold

Men also traveled to the West with dreams of striking it rich. Gold and silver were discovered in Nevada, Colorado, Idaho, and Montana. Men packed into **boomtowns** and spread over the territories searching for their own gold mines. The population of the Colorado Territory grew during the war years.

Central City in the Colorado Territory is pictured here in 1864. The Colorado Territory grew as men hoped to strike it rich there.

Who Protested Slavery in the North?

Slavery had existed in the North since the early years of the colonies. Even though the Declaration of Independence proclaimed all men free, the politicians were afraid to end slavery in 1776. Founding fathers such as George Washington and Thomas Jefferson owned slaves. They both decided slavery was wrong, but felt that declaring freedom from Great Britain was the first, more important job. They hoped that slavery would die out in time. Instead, the invention of the cotton gin meant that **plantation** owners in the South needed even more slaves. The farms of the North were smaller, so slaves were not needed to work the land. Before and after the Civil War, even freed blacks living in the North did not have the same freedoms as white people.

**Primary Source:
Freed Slaves
Attending School**

This photo was taken in 1863 in Arlington, Virginia.

Thinking About the Source:

What do you notice first about the photo?

Think about when the photo was taken. What can you learn from examining it?

Abolitionists

The religious group referred to as the Quakers had spoken out against slavery from the early days of the country. As the disagreements over slavery grew, more people felt that all slaves should be freed. They were called **abolitionists**, because they wanted to abolish, or do away with, slavery.

Frederick Douglass was a slave in Maryland. He borrowed the papers of a freedman and posed as a sailor on a train north. He eventually made it to Massachusetts. Douglass quickly became an active abolitionist. He spoke all over the North, urging the government to put an end to slavery.

A Northern writer, Harriet Beecher Stowe, wrote a book called *Uncle Tom's Cabin*. The book told the story of mistreated slaves in the South. Many readers were inflamed against slavery when they read the book. When President Lincoln met Stowe, he said, "So you're the little woman that made this great war."

Frederick Douglass was a well-known citizen by the end of the Civil War.

The Underground Railroad

Many people felt it was their duty to help escaped slaves rather than give them back to their owners. In 1850, a new **fugitive** slave act was passed by the United States Congress. It stated that people had to do what they could to return escaped slaves to their owners. Slave catchers could capture slaves wherever they found them, even if they were in Northern states where slavery did not exist. Sometimes they kidnapped free blacks and dragged them into slavery. **Abolitionists** were determined to disobey the law and help as many slaves as they could. A system of people and homes open to escaped slaves heading north developed and was called the **Underground Railroad**.

Harriet Tubman was a famous conductor on the Underground Railroad. She escaped from slavery and then returned to help her family and other slaves reach freedom. Her actions led to her nickname of "Moses," after the biblical hero who led his people to freedom.

**Primary Source:
Harriet Tubman**

Harriet Tubman helped many blacks escape slavery using the Underground Railroad.

Thinking About the Source:

When do you think this picture was taken?

Do you think there is anything missing from this picture?

The Thirteenth Amendment

In September 1862, President Lincoln issued the **Emancipation Proclamation**, which would free all slaves in states still in rebellion on January 1, 1863. The war continued, and slaves in the South were not freed until it ended. Finally, on January 31, 1865, Congress passed the Thirteenth Amendment to the **Constitution**, officially ending slavery.

The Thirteenth Amendment put an end to slavery in the United States.

Will These Inventions Work?

Some inventions before and during the Civil War were put to use by the armies. Thaddeus Lowe persuaded the Union army to use hot air balloons to spy on the enemy. After the First Battle of Bull Run, Lowe went up in a balloon and was able to get information on exactly where the troops were.

The USS *Monitor* was an **ironclad** ship built by John Ericsson. The wooden body of the ship was covered with steel plates. During a battle with the Confederate ironclad CSS *Virginia*, both ships suffered little damage because cannonballs bounced off.

The Union army attempted to use hot air balloons to spy on Confederate troop movements.

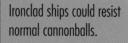

Ironclad ships could resist normal cannonballs.

Photos of Battles

Another advance in technology was photography. Photography had been around only about 20 years when the Civil War began in 1861. George Cook took many photographs of people and battlefields in the South.

Mathew Brady was a famous photographer in the North. He planned to make a photographic history of the war. His own eyesight was failing, so he hired two-man photographic teams to travel to battlefields and take pictures. Brady published the pictures in numbered sets. These photographs survive today to show us the faces of the Civil War and the look of the battlefields.

The Pony Express

Communication was by letter or **telegraph** in the time of the Civil War. California was a Union state separated from the eastern states by the frontier of the Midwest. Telegraph wires were not yet strung across the whole country. Letters sent from the East Coast to California took about a month, sent either by ship around South America or over land by wagon. When it operated from April 1860 to October 1861, the Pony Express delivered mail across the country in about 10 days. Riders would gallop along from station to station, where there were fresh horses and new riders. The fastest ride on record was 7 days and 17 hours, with the bag carrying Lincoln's first **inaugural speech**. The end of the Pony Express came with the completion of telegraph wires across the country.

Primary Source: Mathew Brady

Mathew Brady's photographs give us a vivid picture of what the Civil War was like.

Thinking About the Source:

What, if any, text can you read in this image?

If someone took this picture today, what would be different?

What Were the Words and Music of the Home Front?

Letters galloped across the country with the Pony Express. They also traveled between homes and army camps. Receiving a letter from home was a most welcome treat for a soldier. Sometimes the letter took weeks to arrive. Family members at home also waited eagerly for a letter from their soldier. Mary Strieby of Indiana wrote her husband on September 4, 1865, before he was released from the army, "I have had to work harder than I am able for [since] Sarah Jane has been sick I think is the cause of it, waiting on her and taking care of my baby and doing the work is all most more than I am able for."

News of battles came through the newspapers of the time. When word of a battle leaked out, people gathered at newspaper offices to wait for the **casualty** lists and details about the battle. The newspaper people printed out the names of the wounded and killed, and this was often how families learned the hard news.

Poems and Songs

The times of the Civil War inspired poetry and songs. Walt Whitman wrote a poem about a father and mother receiving a letter from their soldier son, called "Come Up from the Fields, Father."

While the Confederate troops were marching along to "The Bonnie Blue Flag," the Union troops sang "Rally 'Round the Flag." In 1861, Julia Ward Howe took a popular tune and wrote new words. Her song is "The Battle Hymn of the Republic." Another song, "Dixie," is now associated with the South, but it was popular with both armies early in the war and was written by a Northerner.

READING THE WAR NEWS IN BROADWAY, NEW YORK.—FROM A SKETCH BY OUR SPECIAL ARTIST.

Primary Source: Reading the News of War

This is a wood engraving of a crowd waiting for news of the Civil War at a newspaper office on Broadway in New York.

It was created in 1861.

Thinking About the Source:

Why do you think this image was created?

If someone made this today, what would be different?

What Other Effects Did War Have on the Home Front?

At the beginning of the war, the industries of the North felt the loss of Southern cotton, tobacco, and food products. People in the South owed money to businesses in the North, and that money could not be collected once the war started. To make up the losses, Northern businesses raised their prices.

Inflation Hits

The government could no longer collect taxes from the states that **seceded**. To pay for the war supplies and soldiers' salaries, the government printed more money. This made each dollar worth less than before. This process brought on **inflation**, or rising costs. Food, clothes, and wood cost more, but a worker's wages did not increase. **Immigrants** and the poor were hit hardest by inflation because they had no money saved to buy what they needed.

The large number of currencies printed during the war brought on inflation.

Banks in each town could print their own money. But a person had to cash each bill at the bank that issued it. In 1862, Congress passed the Legal Tender Act, which established a national **currency** printed by the U.S. Treasury. The money was guaranteed by the U.S. government and could be used anywhere in the country.

Doing Men's Work

Men from small farms marched off to war, leaving women and boys struggling to plant and harvest crops. A song from the times said, "Just take your gun and go, for Ruth can drive the oxen, John, and I can use the hoe." Women could not easily handle the work required on the farm as well as their own chores of tending the garden and home. They planted smaller crops and worked long hours to care for the fields and animals.

The impact of war was felt on entire families, as men left women behind to struggle with taking care of the home and raising the children. Below, a volunteer for the Union army departs for the war.

People on the home front also worked to support soldiers in the field. Women formed sewing and knitting groups to make uniforms and socks for soldiers. Girls were taught to knit or roll bandages to send to military doctors.

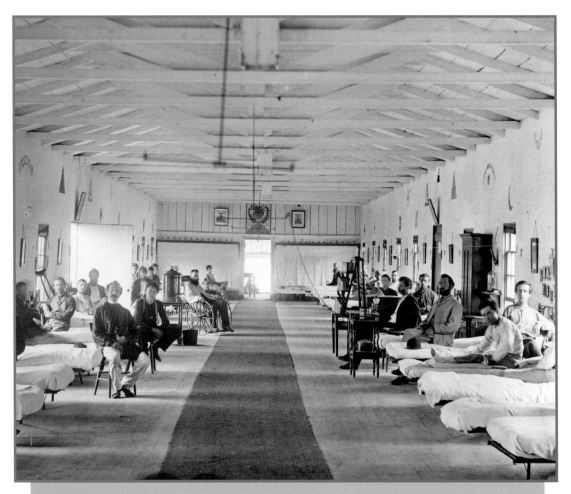

Primary Source:
Washington, D.C. Hospital

Military hospitals always needed more trained nurses and medical supplies.

This is a photograph of a Washington, D.C. hospital taken in 1865.

Thinking About the Source:

What do you notice first about this image?

What people and objects are shown?

How are they arranged?

The Sanitary Commission

Elizabeth Blackwell, the first woman doctor in the country, organized women in New York City into the Women's Central Association of Relief (WCAR). The group collected donations for the army and set up a training system for nurses. In 1861, the government established the U.S. Sanitary Commission, which included the WCAR. Units of the Sanitary Commission were organized across the country.

The Sanitary Commission collected supplies and inspected military hospitals. The organization from Chicago collected donations from the Midwest. In the first two years of the war, the Chicago Commission sent 30,000 boxes of supplies to soldiers in the field. To raise money for transporting the supplies, a large fair was arranged. Donations were collected to be sold at the fair, a dining hall was set up, a parade was arranged, and the fair began. Almost $100,000 was collected.

Commission and Hospital Work

Mary Livermore, director of the Chicago Sanitary Commission, described a typical day's work. She mentioned nurses coming in, soldiers sending requests for a new shirt or something to read, and **civilians** who would "come and go—to visit...to bring news from the hospitals...to make inquiries for missing men, to make donations of money..."

Louisa May Alcott, author of *Little Women*, served as a volunteer nurse during the Civil War. She cared for men with battle wounds, as well as those sick with disease. Her days were spent feeding patients, changing sheets, and giving out medicine. She read letters and newspapers to the patients and wrote letters for those who couldn't do it themselves.

Louisa May Alcott was a nurse during the Civil War. She became famous after *Little Women* was published.

The First Battle of Bull Run

The first major battle of the war, the First Battle of Bull Run, was fought on July 21, 1861. Bull Run is a small creek about 40 kilometers (25 miles) south of Washington, DC. Civilians and government officials joined the march. They thought the Confederates would be quickly beaten and the war ended after one battle.

After several hours of fighting, fresh Confederate troops reached the battlefield and began pushing the tired **Union** troops back. The retreat became a panic, and both Union soldiers and civilians fled in a confused mass. The roads back to Washington, DC, became a traffic jam of carriages and wagons loaded with frightened people. It became known as "the great skedaddle."

The Battle of Antietam

Most of the battles of the Civil War were fought in the South. However, in 1862, Confederate General Robert E. Lee led his troops into Maryland. Union General McClellan planned to push the rebels back into Virginia. They met near Sharpsburg, Maryland, in the Battle of Antietam Creek.

On September 17, the two armies clashed in a battle that lasted 12–13 hours. Nearly 100,000 men fought on the two sides, and more than 23,000 were killed or wounded. This battle caused the highest number of casualties for both sides for one day of the entire war. On September 18, the Confederate army retreated back into Virginia.

CLARA BARTON

Clara Barton nursed men on the battlefield at the Second Battle of Bull Run. She said, "I went in while the battle raged." She was the first nurse to arrive at the Antietam battlefield. She worked during the battle to treat the wounded of both sides with supplies she had brought. At one time, a bullet tore her sleeve as she tended a wounded Confederate soldier. Barton later established the American Red Cross.

People came to watch the First Battle of Bull Run thinking it would be an easy Northern victory.

The Battle of Gettysburg

In June 1863, General Lee again marched his Confederate army north. This time they headed into Pennsylvania, where the opposing armies collided near a small town called Gettysburg.

The Confederate army, led by General Robert E. Lee, had 75,000 men. Union troops, under General George Meade, numbered about 85,000. Through July 1, 2, and 3, they fought around Gettysburg. Once the battle was over, 51,000 men had been killed, wounded, or were missing.

Women, girls, and boys did their best to care for the wounded men who often were shot right outside the doors of their houses. By night of the first day, many houses in Gettysburg had several wounded soldiers sleeping on the floors. Some of these soldiers remained in Gettysburg for weeks before they were healed enough to rejoin the army or travel home.

The Battle of Gettysburg is the bloodiest battle in American history.

Gettysburg Address

Lee's Confederates retreated, and the Union army went on to other battles. The people of Gettysburg surveyed the damage to their town. Over the next few months, they took care of the wounded of both sides and worked to repair the homes, farms, and fences destroyed in the battle. They also buried the dead. A new cemetery was filled with the Union dead.

On November 19, 1863, there was a dedication for the cemetery. The president of Harvard University gave a stirring speech lasting two hours. President Abraham Lincoln spoke only two minutes, but his Gettysburg Address has become one of the most famous speeches in history. He reminded the listeners of the difficulty of forming the country, and that the Civil War was a test of the strength of the Union. He praised the soldiers who fought for freedom. At the end, he said, "that we here highly resolve that these dead shall not have died in vain; that this nation, under God, shall have a new birth of freedom; and that this government of the people, by the people, and for the people, shall not perish from the earth."

**Primary Source:
The Crowd at the
Gettysburg Address**

Lincoln gave his Gettysburg Address on November 19, 1863. It would become one of the most memorable speeches in history.

Thinking About the Source:

What do you notice first about this image?

How does the "crowd" compare to crowds today?

How Did the Civil War End?

By 1865, the Confederacy was almost defeated. Much of the territory of the Confederacy was in the hands of the **Union**. On April 2, the War Department in Washington, DC, received the news that Richmond had fallen. After the Confederate city was captured, Abraham Lincoln went to see the conquered capital.

Union General Ulysses S. Grant was squeezing General Lee's Confederates in every direction. The two armies met near the small village of Appomattox Court House. Grant's army surrounded the Confederates there. Lee knew it was time for him to surrender his Confederate army.

Lee Surrenders

A soldier was sent through the lines with a white flag and a note asking about surrender. Grant replied that he would meet Lee at a home in Appomattox Court House.

Lee (seated left) surrendered to Grant in a nearby house in Appomattox.

When Lee arrived at the home on April 9, 1865, he and Grant talked for a while about a time they had met during the **Mexican-American War**. Grant remembered, "Our conversation grew so pleasant that I almost forgot the object of our meeting." Grant and Lee then signed the surrender papers.

The surrender said that the Confederates would no longer fight against the Union, and that "each officer and man will be allowed to return to his home, not to be disturbed by the United States authorities." Jefferson Davis was captured and jailed for two years. Then he was released and lived to the end of his life in Mississippi.

After the surrender papers were signed, Union troops fired a salute of one hundred guns. Grant spoke, "The war is over. The Rebels are our countrymen again..."

People of the North celebrated Lee's surrender, knowing it meant that the war would end soon. Fireworks and lights lit up the sky in Washington.

Grant (pictured) allowed Lee and the Confederates to surrender with dignity.

Lincoln's Death

Abraham Lincoln had been reelected president of the United States in 1864. Just five days after Lee's surrender, Lincoln attended a play at Ford's Theatre in Washington, DC. Driven by a hatred of the **Union** and a loyalty to the fallen Confederacy, John Wilkes Booth plotted to kill Lincoln, several members of his **cabinet**, and General Grant. He recruited others to take part in the plan. Booth burst into Lincoln's box in the middle of the play and shot him in the back of the head. Soldiers carried Lincoln from the theater to a nearby boardinghouse. The doctors could not save Lincoln, and he died early the next morning. Booth was caught 12 days later on April 26, 1865, but was killed as he tried to escape.

The citizens and soldiers of the North mourned the **assassination** of Lincoln. A teenager who later became a leader for workers, Samuel Gompers, was in New York when the news came. He said, "I remember very vividly the morning that brought the news of President Lincoln's death... It seemed to me that some great power for good had gone out of the world. A master mind had been taken at a time when most needed."

LINCOLN'S SECOND INAUGURAL SPEECH

In his second **inaugural speech** on March 4, 1865, Lincoln spoke about how the people had tried to stop the war and preserve the Union. Now that the war was coming to an end, he begged for **leniency** for the citizens of the South.

The last paragraph of Lincoln's speech said: "With malice toward none, with charity for all, with firmness in the right as God gives us to see the right, let us strive on to finish the work we are in, to bind up the nation's wounds, to care for him who shall have borne the battle and for his widow and his orphan— to do all which may achieve and cherish a just and lasting peace among ourselves and with all nations."

Thousands of people gathered to see Lincoln's funeral train as it made its way from Washington, DC, to Illinois. A portrait of Lincoln was mounted on the front.

Can the Country Be Reunited?

President Andrew Johnson wished to fulfill Lincoln's plan of **leniency** in restoring the Southern states to the **Union**. However, **Radical Republicans** controlled Congress, and they thought it should be more difficult for the rebellious Southern states to rejoin the Union. They tried to **impeach** President Johnson, then placed the South under military occupation. The 11 Southern states that had **seceded** were admitted back into the Union over the next four years. However, the military occupation of the South did not completely end until Rutherford B. Hayes took office as president of the United States in 1877, 12 years after the end of the Civil War.

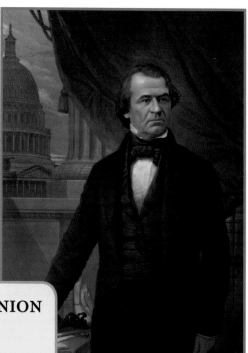

Andrew Johnson became president after Lincoln was assassinated.

STATE	DATE REJOINED THE UNION
Tennessee	July 24, 1866
Arkansas	June 22, 1868
Florida	June 25, 1868
North Carolina	July 4, 1868
Louisiana	July 9, 1868
South Carolina	July 9, 1868
Alabama	July 13, 1868
Virginia	January 26, 1870
Mississippi	February 23, 1870
Texas	March 30, 1870
Georgia	July 15, 1870

The Southern states rejoined the Union.

Freedom for Slaves

The end of the war brought freedom to the slaves of the South. But they had no money or land, so survival was difficult. Many agreed to work for their former masters, becoming sharecroppers. Others traveled north to try to find work. Racial tensions were strong, so many former slaves were still mistreated. The Freedman's Bureau was created to help blacks establish farms, learn to read, and start businesses.

Soldiers Come Home

Union soldiers and businessmen returned home. Families rejoiced to have the men home again. Men went back to work in their businesses and on their farms.

Other families faced the sorrow of men not returning. An estimated 620,000 men from both the North and South were killed and another 470,000 were wounded during the Civil War. A large number of the returning men were disabled and could not work, so their families continued to run the farms and businesses.

Freed slaves still faced a struggle to survive after the war.

The Union secretary of war convinced President Andrew Johnson to have a grand review of the Union army. It took two days for 150,000 soldiers to march along the Washington streets, past the Capitol. The building was draped in black to honor the fallen soldiers and the assassinated President Lincoln.

People of the North left the war behind and began to build industries, businesses, and farms. The returning soldiers felt that great opportunities and a chance for wealth were available for anyone who was ready to work.

Many people from both North and South decided to build their lives in the West. An addition to the Homestead Act gave veterans an advantage. They could claim the land after living on it only one year. For each year after the war, as many as 5 to 7 million acres were homesteaded.

Troops marched in ceremony through Washington, DC, after the war.

The transcontinental railroad was a major advancement for transportation and shipping.

The First Transcontinental Railroad

The first transcontinental railroad was completed after the war. On May 10, 1869, a symbolic gold spike was driven into the rails at Promontory, Utah. A person could travel across the country by train, and many traveled west to new farms and businesses.

The tensions left from the Civil War took a long time to heal. Memorial Day was established to honor those who died in the Civil War, as well as from other wars. Soldiers from both sides eventually reunited in memory.

The Civil War was over. Slavery was abolished, and the states were reunited into one country. The nation pushed forward into prosperity for the North, and eventually the conditions in the South improved for the people. The divisions of the war faded, and the country faced the world as a united whole.

Timeline

1820	Missouri Compromise
1850	Compromise of 1850
1854	Kansas-Nebraska Act
1860	Abraham Lincoln elected president of the United States
December 1860– May 1861	Eleven Southern states secede from the Union
February 1861	Jefferson Davis appointed president of the Confederacy
April 12, 1861	Confederate forces attack Fort Sumter, beginning the Civil War
July 21, 1861	First Battle of Bull Run, or Manassas
September 1862	Lincoln signs the Emancipation Proclamation
March 9, 1862	Battle of ironclads CSS *Virginia* and USS *Monitor*
July 4, 1863	General Grant captures Vicksburg after a long siege
February 17, 1864	The CSS *H.L Hunley* sinks the USS *Housatonic* and then also sinks

September 2, 1864   General Sherman takes Atlanta

December 21, 1864   Sherman captures Savannah

April 9, 1865   General Robert E. Lee surrenders to General Grant

April 15, 1865   President Lincoln dies after being shot by John Wilkes Booth

January 31, 1865   Thirteenth Amendment to the Constitution ends slavery

Glossary

abolitionist during the Civil War period, a person who wanted to end slavery in the United States

assassination murder of a prominent person, usually for political reasons

Black Hawk War war fought between the state militia and Native Americans of the Illinois region over disputed land

boomtown town that has experienced rapid growth, usually due to a gold strike

cabinet people who advise the leader of the government and help make important decisions

cash crop crop such as tobacco, rice, or cotton that is grown in large amounts to be sold for cash

casualty loss in a battle, including a soldier wounded, killed, or missing

census official count of a country's population

civilian any person who is not in active duty in the military

compromise agreement achieved after everyone involved accepts less than they originally wanted

Confederate States of America group of 11 Southern states that seceded from the United States in 1860-1861

Constitution fundamental law of the United States that went into effect in 1789

currency money

draft requirement to serve in the military

economic referring to the financial system

economy system of economic activity, including commerce for producing, selling, and buying goods and services

Emancipation Proclamation document issued by President Lincoln that granted freedom to slaves living in Confederate states when those states did not return to the Union by January 1, 1863

fugitive runaway slave; person wanted by legal authorities

General Assembly group of lawmakers for a state

immigrant person who comes to live in a new country

inaugural speech talk given by the president at his swearing-in ceremony; also called the inaugural address

inflation situation where money is worth less and prices are rising

ironclad warship covered with iron plates

leniency generosity or mercy

Mexican-American War conflict between the United States and Mexico from 1846 to 1848

militia nonprofessional military group that takes orders from a state

plantation large farm or estate that is worked by a large number of laborers, like slaves

Radical Republicans Republican members of Congress at the end of the Civil War who tried to impeach Andrew Johnson and make it harder for Southern states to rejoin the Union

Revolutionary War war against the British for American independence, fought 1775–1783

secede break away from something

sod bricks of grass with the soil attached

states' rights rights and powers the states possess in relation to the federal government, as guaranteed by the Constitution

surrender quit a battle, admitting defeat

telegraph method of communication where dots and dashes (Morse code) is sent over wires

tenement crowded apartment house, usually home to the poor

Underground Railroad network of secret routes used to help slaves escape the South to gain freedom

Union United States of America

U.S. House of Representatives lower body of the law-making branch (Congress) of the U.S. government

U.S. Senate upper body of lawmakers of the U.S. government, which has fewer members who serve longer terms than members of the House of Representatives

veteran person who has served in the military

Find Out More

Books

Arnold, James R. *The Civil War*. Minneapolis, MN: Lerner Publishing, 2005.

Doeden, Matt. *The Civil War*. Mankato, MN: Capstone Press, 2010.

Flynn, Claire E. *Causes and Effects of the American Civil War*. New York: Rosen Publishing, 2009.

Hama, Larry. *The Battle of Antietam*. New York: Rosen Publishing, 2007.

Websites

http://www.gettysbg.com/battle.shtml
This is the website for the Gettysburg Welcome Center.

http://www.suffolk.lib.ny.us/youth/jccivil.html
This site, from the Suffolk County, NY, library contains kid-friendly links to more information on the Civil War.

DVDs

Civil War: America Divided (DVD). Mill Creek Entertainment, 2008.

Index

abolitionists 21, 22

Alcott, Louisa May 31

American Red Cross 32

Appomattox Court House, Virginia 36–37

Barton, Clara 32

Battle of Antietam 32

Battle of Bull Run (First) 24, 32

Battle of Bull Run (Second) 32

Battle of Gettysburg 34

Blackwell, Elizabeth 31

Booth, John Wilkes 38

Brady, Mathew 25

Calhoun, John C. 6

children 12, 14, 16, 29, 34

Clay, Henry 6

communication 25

Compromise of 1850 6

Confederate army 24, 26, 32, 34, 35, 36, 37

Confederate States of America 6

Cook, George 25

cotton 12, 14, 20, 28

crime 16

CSS Virginia 24

Davis, Jefferson 37

deaths 11, 16, 26, 32, 34, 38, 41, 43

Democratic Party 6

diseases 16, 31

Douglass, Frederick 21

Douglas, Stephen 9

economy 4, 6, 28–29

elections 6, 8, 9, 10, 38

Emancipation Proclamation 23

Ericsson, John 24

escapes 22, 38

factories 5, 14

farming 4, 5, 12, 16, 18, 19, 20, 29, 35, 41, 42, 43

Freedman's Bureau 41

frontier regions 8, 18, 19, 25

Gettysburg Address 35

Gompers, Samuel 38

Grant, Ulysses S. 10, 36, 37, 38

Homestead Act (1862) 18, 42

hot air balloons 24

Howe, Julia Ward 26

immigrants 4, 5, 16, 28

inflation 28

ironclads 24

jobs 4, 16

Johnson, Andrew 10, 40, 42

Kansas-Nebraska Act 6

knitting groups 30

Lee, Robert E. 32, 34, 35, 36, 37

Legal Tender Act (1862) 29

letters 25, 26, 31

Lincoln, Abraham 6, 8, 9, 10, 11, 21, 23, 25, 35, 36, 38, 40, 42

Lincoln, Mary Todd 11

Livermore, Mary 31

Lowe, Thaddeus 24

machinery 12, 14, 20

McClellan, George 32

McCormick, Cyrus 12

military hospitals 30, 31

mining 5, 19

Missouri Compromise (1820) 6

money 28–29, 31

newspapers 26, 27, 31

nurses 30, 31, 32

photography 25

poetry 26

Pony Express 25, 26

population 5, 16, 19

railroads 43

Republican Party 6, 40

secession 4, 5, 6, 8, 10, 28, 40

shipping industry 15

slavery 4, 6, 8, 14, 20, 21, 22, 23, 41, 43

songs 26, 29

spying 24

states' rights 4, 5

Stowe, Harriet Beecher 21

Strieby, Mary 26

supplies 4, 28, 30, 31, 32

surrender 36–37

taxes 28

telegraphs 24, 25

tenements 16, 17

Thirteenth Amendment 23

transcontinental railroad 43

Tubman, Harriet 22

Underground Railroad 22

Union army 4, 16, 19, 24, 26, 32, 34, 35, 36, 37, 41, 42

U.S. Congress 6, 9, 10, 18, 22, 23, 29, 40

U.S. Constitution 8, 23

U.S. Sanitary Commission 31

USS Monitor 24

U.S. Treasury 29

veterans 42, 43

wagon trains 19

Webster, Daniel 6

Whitman, Walt 26

women 12, 14, 29, 30, 31, 34